IMAGES
of Aviation

BEECHCRAFT

Walter H. Beech and a Travel Air B6C biplane with a 160hp Curtiss C-6A engine. Mr Beech flew Travel Airs to first place in the 1925 Tulsa Air Race and 1926 Ford Civil Aircraft Reliability Tour.

IMAGES
of Aviation

BEECHCRAFT

Compiled by
Ken Wixey

TEMPUS

First published 1999
Copyright © Ken Wixey, 1999

Tempus Publishing Limited
The Mill, Brimscombe Port,
Stroud, Gloucestershire, GL5 2QG

ISBN 0 7524 1617 0

Typesetting and origination by
Tempus Publishing Limited
Printed in Great Britain by
Midway Clark Printing, Wiltshire

Beech C-45 No.1391 of the Canadian Armed Forces (Reserve). This 1950s close-up shows its 450hp Pratt & Whitney Wasp Junior engines and landing gear details.

Contents

Acknowledgements 6

Introduction 7

1. W.H. Beech, Travel Air and the Staggerwing 9

2. The First Twin Beech Family 19

3. Beech Singles and more Twins 39

4. Sky Queen – The Beech Queen Airs 73

5. Of Barons, Dukes and Kings 85

6. Skyliners and a Starship 125

Acknowledgements

The author would like to express his sincere gratitude for the help rendered in the preparation of this book. A compilation of photographs in this context is reliant on official company archives, personal collections and commercially available lists of aviation subjects. Therefore I am indebted to Phyllis J. McCabe of Corporate Affairs, Raytheon Aircraft (Beech/Hawker), Wichita, Kansas, for providing many of the official Beechcraft photographs. I am also very grateful to Brian Pickering (MAP) and Brian Stainer (APN) for permission to use prints from their respective lists and likewise to Roger Wasley for help from his private collection. For much of the detailed information on Beech aircraft, I must also thank the Raytheon Company for an appreciable variety of technical and historical files freely provided during recent years. References were also made to that excellent publication by Putnam, *Beech Aircraft and their Predecessors* by A.J. Pelletier.

Introduction

Beechcraft – A tradition of excellence

On 30 January 1891 a son was born to Cornelius and Tommie (Hay) Beech at Pulaski, Tennessee. Named Walter Herschel Beech, he was to become a pioneer in the field of aviation. At fourteen years of age he built a glider from bed sheets and wood, his attempt to fly it abruptly ending the glider's career. Even so, he became enthused with flying and on 11 July 1914 made his first solo flight from near Minneapolis in a Curtiss pusher biplane, an aircraft acquired by Beech and a friend as a wreck before its repair and assembly in Walter Beech's home workshop.

In 1917 W.H. Beech joined the US Army Signal Corps Aviation Section and was assigned to Kelly Field, Texas, as a flying instructor. After the war he continued as an Army instructor, receiving an honourable discharge in June 1920. By then, barnstorming and exhibition flying was focusing public interest in aviation and W.H. Beech was soon visiting most states flying war-surplus Curtiss J-4 Jenny trainers. This gave him valuable insight into flying techniques and design that would guide him in his future career.

By 1921, the Wichita-based Laird company was developing a three-seat, tandem, open-cockpit biplane named the Swallow and Beech became their test pilot and demonstrator. He flew the Swallow at national air meetings and won the first of many trophies which he would receive for his prowess in aerobatics and air racing.

Laird reorganized in 1923 to form the Swallow Airplane Manufacturing Company and W.H. Beech was put in charge of all field work. Before long, as his efforts in design and sales gained importance, Beech became vice-president and general manager. When the company president wanted a wooden fuselage for a new Swallow design, however, Beech opposed it in favour of a metal structure. The argument ended with Beech and his supporters resigning from Swallow. To prove the advantages of metal airframes, Beech organized a new Wichita-based aircraft company in an old planing mill and produced a three-seat, open-cockpit biplane powered by a Curtiss OX-5 engine. This appeared in 1925 and was named the Travel Air.

Thereafter, Walter Beech led the Travel Air Manufacturing Co. to produce aircraft containing the latest equipment and design advantages. One result was the famous Model 5000 Travel Air, the first design built to airline specifications and the first type in National Air Transport's (NAT) airline fleet to operate day and night services between Chicago and Dallas. In order to encourage air travel, Beech took part in numerous air meets and races piloting Travel Airs, one of his more noted feats being to win the 1926 Ford Commercial Airplane Reliability Tour, a demonstration of flying 'blind' on Pioneer instruments. In a Travel Air with navigator Brice Goldsborough, Beech led over forty entrants in a twelve-day tour of fourteen US cities to win the $7,000 Edsel Ford Trophy. He also added the J.H. Turner Trophy and Flint Air Meet Successful Winner to his triumphs.

After building more than 200 biplanes, Travel Air turned out its first monoplanes in 1927. They were an immediate success. Their reputation was enhanced with the winning of the 1927 Dole Air Derby by the Travel Air 5000 cabin monoplane *Woolaroc* of the Phillips Petroleum Company, which went from Oakland, California, to Wheeler Field, Hawaii, flown by Art Goebel and William Davis, to win the $25,000 first prize. For the 1929 air race season, W.H. Beech and the Travel Air team produced the Model R, which became known as the 'Mystery S.' A stubby, low-wing monoplane, this racer had a top speed of 235mph and was entered in the National Air Race's fifty-mile Thompson Trophy closed-course free-for-all. The aircraft won at an average speed of 194.9mph piloted by Doug Davis. It was the first time that a civilian aircraft had defeated military machines in a speed competition. Travel Airs became extremely popular and in 1929 the company built 1,000 machines, making Travel Air the world's largest producer of both biplane and monoplane commercial aircraft. Then, late in 1929, Travel Air merged with Curtiss-Wright, W.H. Beech becoming president of Curtiss-Wright Airplane Company and vice-president in charge of sales at the Curtiss-Wright Corporation.

In 1930 Walter Beech married Olive Ann Mellor, who had been his secretary and office manager at Travel Air. However, Beech found much of his work necessitated being in New York and, deciding against the life of a big city executive, he reverted to designing and building aircraft, resigning from Curtiss-Wright in 1932. W.H. Beech and his wife returned to Wichita with a small group of employees from Travel Air and in April 1932 the Beech Aircraft Company was formed. Working in part of a depression-closed factory, Walter Beech insisted they would build only the finest aircraft, their first objective being the design and building of a five-seat, closed-cabin biplane with a top speed of 200mph but containing the luxury and comfort of a fine sedan car. Hours of hard work were rewarded on 4 November 1932, when the first Beechcraft Model 17R biplane emerged. This design was unorthodox in featuring the aerodynamic features of a negative stagger wing, but the aircraft lived up to all expectations and when owned by the Ethyl Corporation, won the Texaco Trophy at the Miami Air Races in January 1933. A year later Beech Aircraft moved back to its old Travel Air factory and the Beech 17 Staggerwing became an aviation classic.

On 15 January 1937 the twin-engine Beech Model 18 made its first flight and was an immediate success, with many civil and military variants following. The last Model 18 was delivered in 1969 after some 9,000 had been built. In the meantime the four-seat Model 35 Bonanza of 1945, with its distinguished V-tail, was to prove most popular during the post-war years both in the US and abroad. It would be followed by updated Bonanza variants plus a Twin-Bonanza and Mentor single-engine military trainer which also sold well. A whole series of new Beech designs were to appear in the next three decades, suiting both commercial and military demands.

Sadly the man responsible for the great success of Beechcraft did not see the fulfillment of his dreams. Walter H. Beech died of a heart attack on the evening of 29 November 1950 at a time when his company had a backlog of $50 million for military production on its books. His widow, Olive Beech, took over the reigns of a company her husband had made famous throughout the aviation world, outliving him by some forty-three years. Olive Ann Beech died on 6 July 1993.

In his time W.H. Beech had developed, or helped develop, eighty types of aircraft and amassed some 10,000 hours of flying time. The greatest tribute to Walter H. Beech must be the thousands of square feet of Beechcraft factory buildings and offices which exist in the United States, as well as the many types of modern Beechcrafts flying in the western world today. When you see a turboprop, twin-engined, executive type private aircraft flying over, or observe those parked up on civil airports you can guarantee, with few exceptions, they are Beechcraft designs. This alone is a monument to the vision and pioneering spirit of one man. As long as there are aircraft and men to fly them the memory of Walter H. Beech will live on in aviation circles.

One
W.H. Beech, Travel Air and the Staggerwing

This was the Travel Air Model 5000, a five-seat cabin monoplane built to airline specifications. It was the first model in the National Air Transport fleet, flying day and night between Chicago and Dallas.

Travel Air Model No.1, which first flew in March 1925 powered by a 90hp Curtiss OX-5 engine. It is flying here near Wichita piloted by W.H. Beech, who later sold it to an O.E. Scott.

In 1926 the Travel Air 4000 open cockpit three-seater emerged. This B-4000 update had a new type of landing gear, a revised wing layout and a 200hp Wright Whirlwind J-5C. Note the strut-mounted landing light.

Former Travel Air engineer Walter Burnham designed this Curtiss Wright CW-15D Sedan after Travel Air became part of Curtiss Wright. A four-seat cabin monoplane, it was powered by a 240hp Wright Whirlwind J-6-7 radial, seen here with a ring cowling fitted.

The winner of the August 1927 Dole Race from Oakland, California, to Hawaii, this was the Travel Air *Woolaroc*, which then had a 230hp Wright Whirlwind J-5-C engine. Here it has a 400hp Pratt & Whitney fitted, the front cockpit removed and large windows installed.

A portrait of Walter H. Beech, co-founder of Beech Aircraft Corporation, who was determined to build and sell the best aircraft possible. He certainly achieved his purpose as the thousands of Beechcraft flying in today's skies bear testimony.

When W.H. Beech was asked to produce an aircraft for the 1929 air racing season that would outfly any other in its class, the Travel Air Model R was built in great secrecy, becoming known as the 'Mystery Ship'. A low wing, open cockpit monoplane with fixed, spatted, landing gear, it was powered by a 425hp Wright J-6-9 radial. It won the first Thompson Trophy Race at the Cleveland National Air Races in 1929 flown by Douglas Davis at an average speed of 194.96mph. In this free-for-all contest, it was the first time a civil machine had beaten the military entrants, a Curtiss P-36A coming second.

The first aircraft built by Beechcraft, the Model 17 prototype (NC499) with a 420hp Wright R-975-E2 Whirlwind engine. It first flew on 4 November 1932 and in January 1933 won the Texaco Trophy in the Miami Air Races. The fixed, 'trousered' landing gear contained electric motors which partially retracted the wheels in flight. Here, modifications include a wider-track landing gear, a fully swivelling tailwheel and narrow-chord flaps prior to the aircraft being sold to the Ethyl Corporation in April 1934.

A 1935 Beech B17R, with a 420hp Wright R-975-E2/E3, an 8ft 6in diameter Hamilton propeller and featuring blind-flying instruments. This British-registered B17R, G-ADLE, in floatplane configuration, made a 1935 World Flight piloted by F.L. Farquhar.

A 1937 Beech D17A, of which ten were built, with a longer fuselage, a cantilever tailplane and upper wing ailerons. Like all Model 17s after the prototype, a fully retracting landing gear was standard. NC19453 seen here later became a US Army UC-43F.

Attached to the American Embassy in London, this Beech D17S is seen under evaluation by the US Army as a YC-43 in 1938. With a 450hp Pratt & Whitney Wasp Junior, it later went to the RAF as DR628.

Ten Beech D17Ss and eight D17s were acquired by the US Navy from civil sources to become GB-1s before it purchased seven GB-1s directly in 1939 and a further three in 1940. Seen here is BuNo 1898, first of the 1940 trio. GB-1s had a 400hp Pratt & Whitney R-985-48 engine.

Here a formation of US Navy Beech GB-2s show off the type's distinguished outline. These five-seat staff transports, with 450hp Pratt & Whitney R-985-AN1s, had a top speed of 205mph. Named 'Travellers', a number of GB-2s arrived in Britain under the Lend-Lease system.

The Model F17D was introduced in 1938 with a 330hp, seven-cylinder Jacobs L-6 (R-915) radial engine and an 8ft 3in diameter Hamilton Standard adjustable or controllable-pitch, two-blade propeller. At a price of $13,980 each, sixty-one Beech F17Ds were built.

This Beech UC-43BH Traveller (43-10828) was from an early batch of seventy-five ordered for the US Army Air Corps (USAAC) as a four/five-seat light transport and utility aircraft. Its engine was a 450hp Pratt & Whitney R-985-AN-1 Wasp Junior. The US Navy received sixty-three as GB-1s.

The first production Beech G17S of 1946 (NC80302), an update of the D17S with revised cowling, windscreen, exhaust system, elevators, instrument panel, etc. Note the large US insignia: this aircraft went to the West Indies Sugar Corporation, Dominican Republic.

The cockpit interior and instrument panel of a 1946 Beech G17S. The instruction to the right of the control column reads: 'When one or more passengers are carried right front seat must be occupied.'

The last D17S built, NC21934, is seen here after it was modified by Beech as the G17S. The new-style windscreen and B drag-reducing cowling for the 450hp Pratt & Whitney R-985-AN4 Wasp Junior radial are apparent. The top speed of the G17S was 212mph and the range 1,000 miles.

Two
The First
Twin Beech Family

This was the prototype Beech Model 18 (NC15810), medium-size passenger transport, which possessed an excellent performance for the feeder lines and charter work for which W.H. Beech intended it. His design team, led by Ted A. Wells, concentrated on low operating cost, cabin comfort and high safety standards. The Beech 18 would need to operate from small airfields, be extremely reliable and be easy to maintain. Power was provided by two 350hp Wright R-760-E2 Whirlwind radial engines. The prototype is seen here on a test flight in January 1937.

One of the initial production batch of Beech Model 18Ds that emerged in 1938, this is NC1284. In this case power was provided by a pair of 330hp Jacob L-6 radials. The Model S18D could be fitted with alternative float or ski landing gear.

A number of military versions of the Beech 18 were produced, this being a US Navy JRB-2 (BuNo 4725). It was one of fifteen ordered by the Navy as six-seater light transports, five of which were transferred UC-45s from the USAAF. Engines were 450hp Pratt & Whitney R-985-50s or AN4 Wasp Juniors.

Some Beech 18s served as AT-7 Navigators, a USAAF navigational trainer housing three separate chart tables and equipment. A rotatable astrodome was located atop the fuselage just behind the cockpit. This 1941 photograph shows a USAAC AT-7 coded N54.

Designed for bombardier and gunnery training, the Beech AT-11 Kansan was a military version of the 18S. Up to 1000lb of bombs could be carried in a small bomb bay and a twin-gun dorsal turret was often fitted. With the latter removed, thirty-six AT-11s converted as AT-11A navigation trainers. Power was provided by two 450hp Pratt & Whitney Wasp Junior engines. Note the Plexiglas bomb aiming nose.

Overleaf: The US Navy's Beech JRB-1 variant was designed for directing radio-controlled target aircraft and, for this reason, had the large fairing seen here above the cockpit to provide the radio-control operator with a good field of view in all directions.

This particular JRB-1 of the US Navy, pictured in 1940, is serialled BuNo 2543. It was the first Beech Model 18 variant acquired by the Navy. The cupola above the cockpit for drone guidance purposes gives an unusual profile to the type.

The final production model of the UC-45 was the UC-45F, with seven seats and a slightly longer nose. Of 1,522 built for the USAAF, forty-two were F-2B special photographic versions, while 343 went to the Navy as JRB-3s and JRB-4s. This is a USAAF UC-45F, 44-47462/'7870'.

Of some 9,000 Beech Model 18s built, large numbers were produced in the Second World War as advanced military trainers and transports for Allied use (Beech built 1,582 AT-11 Kansans alone for the USAAF, while the US Navy would receive over 1,500 JRB or SNB variants). This 1941 photograph shows Walter H. Beech and his wife, Olive Ann Beech, joint founders of Beech Aircraft Corporation, overlooking military Model 18 production at Wichita.

Several Allied Air Forces flew the basic personnel and liaison variant of the Beech 18 (what the USAAF called the UC-45A and the US Navy, the JRB-1). Many served with Britain's Royal Air Force and Royal Navy service as the Expeditor. This machine, No.326/'KH', is seen in Royal Canadian Air Force service in the 1950s.

With a modified half-glazed nose section but still powered by the trusty 450hp Pratt & Whitney R-985 Wasp Juniors, this Beech AT-11 Kansan (No.2503) is in Portuguese Air Force service in the 1960s.

This Twin Beech, one of a number of JRB-4/SNB-5s delivered to the French Navy (Aeronavale) carries serial 51103/'3' and is fitted with updated radar and avionics.

The Italian Air Force acquired a number of C-45s in 1949 as an interim measure, intending to fly them for up to three years. In fact they lasted until the 1980s. This Italian machine is MM61676/'RR-41'.

The first British-registered Twin Beech, G-AIYI, an 18S (ex-USAAF 42-43477; Royal Navy FE883). As a luxury conversion for Prince Aly Khan, it is seen here waiting for Customs clearance at Croydon in May 1949. Sadly, on 24 August of the same year, this aircraft crashed at Sherburn-in-Elmet, Yorkshire.

It was decided in 1951 to upgrade existing C-45Fs, RC-45As, AT-7s and AT-11s to C-45G standard. Beech carried out the modifications which included new strengthened centre sections, longer nacelles, new landing gear legs, wheels, brakes and instrument panel, A-3A autopilot, Pratt & Whitney R-985-AN-3 engines and constant-speed, fully feathering propellers. In this photograph, the rebuilt C-45G No.51-11495 of the United States Air Force shows off its pleasing lines.

A number of Beech 18s served in the Royal Canadian Air Force during the days of Lend-Lease in the Second World War and well into the post-war years. In this 1953 aerial shot is Beech C-45 No.1534/'AO-N' of No.412 Squadron, RCAF.

A number of original US Navy Beech SNB-2s converted to SNB-2P photo-reconnaissance were in turn rebuilt to SNB-5P standard. Survivors in 1962 became RC-45Js like this one, BuNo 29645, seen here in 1967 at the Naval Air Station, Alameda.

The Beech 18 was designed to provide a twin float landing gear option, which made it very popular in Canada. Here, with its port Wasp Junior engine uncowled for maintenance, is Beech D18S floatplane CF-VCC of Hooker Air Service (Canada) in 1975.

Another Beech D18S in floatplane configuration, in this case CF-OII of the Canadian company Ignace Airways Ltd. Note the sturdy float struts, fixed entrance ladders and ventral fin, fitted to enhance stability in flight.

On 26 April 1946 Beechcraft's D18S became the first post-war commercial aircraft to receive a US Government type certificate. A deluxe executive version of the military Twin Beech, it had a higher gross weight and increased range and payload. This D18S carries US civil registration NC44592.

Civil Beech Model 18s, whether ex-military or newly built, served in many countries, often on charter work or with short-haul secondary airlines. This machine (OB-LJB/'504') was photographed in the 1970s when operating with Solar Airways S.A. of Peru.

The first of the Super Twin Beech series, the E18S, was introduced in 1954 with expanded cabin area, squared wingtip extensions, a 9,300lb gross weight and executive-style seating for ten. Shown here is an E18S with US registration N3460B. The improvements in design and profile are apparent in this picture.

This Beech Model 18S, carrying Dutch registration PH-LPS, is pictured at Britain's Blackbushe airport in 1956. Power was again provided by two Pratt & Whitney Wasp Junior engines.

The 1959 Beech G18S retained the horsepower, cruising speed and gross weight of the Super E18S but had a new windscreen, a large centre cabin window and three-blade propellers. This G18S is registered N9933R.

A tricycle landing gear and extended nose section were optional on the Beech H18 of 1962. Seating was provided for ten persons, while updates included revised landing gear legs and wheels, electric cowling flaps, air conditioning and increased fuel capacity. Here US-registered N422X taxies past the camera.

From 1959 Volpar Inc. produced Beech 18 tricycle landing gear conversion kits. The retractable nose wheel was housed in a redesigned streamlined nose, increasing the fuselage length of the Tri-gear by 28in. Pictured is Tri-gear N99032 of Sierra Pacific Airlines.

The Volpar conversion resulted in the main landing gear being moved 4ft further aft to retract forward into the nacelle. The longer nose could also house a 12in radar scanner. In this 1970s shot Beech H18 Tri-gear P-2022 serves with the Indonesian Police.

Still powered by a pair of 450hp Pratt & Whitney R-985-AN14B Wasp Juniors, this Beech H18 Tri-gear (N24H), with Volpar conversion apparent, is shown in the 1960s when operated by Hawaii Pacific Airlines.

The port entry door and steps are clearly visible on this Beech 18 Tri-gear as it basks in the sun, the R-985 Wasp Junior engines at rest. Photographed in 1965, N187R was then operated by Air Taxis Inc. The outer port wing leading-edge appears to have been removed, presumably for maintenance purposes.

This Beech/Hamilton-Westwind III, a D18S conversion, was powered by two 579hp Pratt & Whitney Canada PT6A-20 turboprops. Note the streamline nose extension, revised nacelles and ventral fin. N23ILJ was serving with Connie Kalitta Services when seen here in the 1970s.

Here a Beech/Volpar Tri-gear has been fitted with 575shp Garrett TPE-331-25 turboprops and leading-edge extensions to increase tankage. Over twenty were converted thus as Volpar Turbo 18s. Shown here is N9231 of Arabesco Airlines.

Three Beech Model 25/USAAC AT-10 Wichita two-seat advanced trainers of 1941. Powered by two 295hp Lycoming R-680-9 radials, they were built mainly of wood and became standard equipment in USAAF Advanced Training Schools for multi-engine pilots.

USAAF Beech trainers in the 1940s: an AT-10 Wichita 42-2289 (nearest), AT-7 Navigator 43-33278 (centre) and AT-11 Kansan 42-37292. The two-seat AT-10 Wichitas had wooden fuel tanks lined with synthetic rubber!

Responding to USAAF requirements in 1942 for a two-seat attack bomber, Beechcraft produced their XA-38 Grizzly. Two prototypes were built (43-14406/07) as seen here, powered by two 2,300hp Wright GR-3350-43 Cyclones. They flew on May 7 1944 and 22 September 1945 respectively, but with the Second World War nearing its end the XA-38 did not reach production status.

The Beech XA-38 Grizzly was designed to knock-out enemy bombers, ground positions and armour. It was armed with a 75mm nose-mounted cannon – clearly visible here – augmented by six 0.50in guns, two in the nose and two each in upper and lower remote-control turrets. Its underwing stores could carry bombs, depth charges, smoke screen tanks, napalm, torpedoes or extra fuel tanks.

Three
Beech Singles
and more Twins

Walter H. Beech wanted to build an aircraft in 1945 which could carry four persons and their luggage in car-style comfort at 180mph. He achieved this with the Beech 35 Bonanza, first flown in December 1945. This British-registered A35 Bonanza (G-ASIZ) has a 185hp Continental E-185-1 engine.

A distinguishing feature of the Model 35 Bonanza was its 'Butterfly' V-tail, seen clearly in this view of N9135S, a US-registered V35B Bonanza with a 285hp Continental 10-520-BA fuel-injected engine. A three-blade Hartzell propeller was optional.

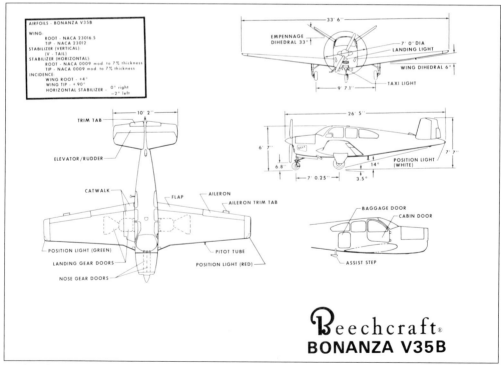

A plan drawing of the V35B Bonanza showing the distinctive V-tail.

When the Model N35 Bonanza was introduced in 1961 it had a new, larger third cabin window installed and a 260hp Continental 10-470-N engine, here with an optional three-blade Hartzell propeller. This is a French-registered N35 Bonanza (F-BNOL) pictured in 1967. The V-tail is prominent in this view.

Six passengers could be carried in the S35 Bonanza of 1964, which had its fuselage lengthened by 19in. Power was provided by a 285hp Continental 10-520-B engine. Note the position of the flaps and elevators on British-registered G-ATII in its landing configuration.

First flown on 14 September 1959, the Beech Model 33 Debonair was a four-seat, single-engine executive aircraft. A conventional swept-tailed variant of the Model 35 Bonanza, it was powered by a 225hp Continental 10-470-J/K. Shown here in 1970 is a Swiss-registered A33 Debonair, HB-EKL.

The updating carried out on the B33 Debonair, introduced in 1961, included new instrument panels, adjustable backs to the front seats, small fin fairing, stall-warning horn and leading-edge tanks (optional) to provide an extra twenty-nine US gallons of fuel. This 1967 photo shows French-registered B33 Debonair F-BMSC with a 225hp Continental 10-470-K engine.

The Model C33 Debonair of 1965 featured an extended dorsal fin fairing, adjustable backs for the rear seats, a larger third cabin window (optional) and a 225hp Continental 10-470-K engine. This British-registered C33 Debonair (G-AVHG) was newly imported in 1968 and is pictured here in 1971.

The Beech Model E33 appeared in 1968 as a Bonanza. It retained a Continental 10-470-K, but standard fuel tanks contained fifty US gallons (eighty US gallon tanks were optional). A larger, new style windscreen was also installed and the third cabin window was standard. This French-registered E33A Bonanza (F-BRIZ) was similar but had a 285hp Continental 10-520-B engine.

Something akin to the earlier Bonanza V35B, an F33A Bonanza appeared in 1970 with a 285hp Continental 10-520-BA. Short and long fuselage versions were built, twenty-six of the former in 1970. This short body Bonanza F33A carries US registration N9133S.

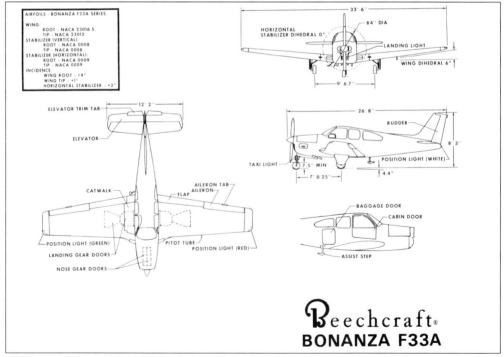

This plan of the F33A, published in 1978, reveals its similarity to the V35B. The vertical tail has a very different look from the 'Butterfly' V-tail, however.

A long fuselage Beech F33A Bonanza (N6679B), a type still in production during the mid-1990s. A 19in fuselage extension allowed six-seat accommodation and a larger baggage door, which was further enlarged on the 1985 version. A three-blade propeller was then fitted and super soundproofing installed.

Spain received fifty-four Beech F33A and F33C Bonanzas for the Spanish Air Force as E.24As and E.24Bs respectively. Here E.24-13 is pictured in 1989 with Ala 42 as aircraft number 12. E.24As also operated with Escuadron 791 of the Academia General del Aire.

The Beech A36 Bonanza series, an updated version of the 1968 Model 36, was further improved to include a 300hp Continental 10-550-B engine, a new instrument panel, added interior luxury, new wingtips, vortex generators and quick-release cowling latches. Here Bonanza A36 N1836F flies over rugged USA terrain.

The instrument panel installation facing the pilot of a Beech A36 Bonanza. In 1972 vertical readout engine instruments had been made standard; later updates included a 24-volt electric system, four-second landing gear retract/extend time and avionics to include a King KX-170B 720-channel nav/com, with KI-201C VOR/LOC Omni conv/ind plus Beech antenna.

Beech A36 Bonanza variants sold well in America and abroad, including Australia, Finland, Germany, the Netherlands, Japan and Saudi Arabia. Here N9136S, an American-registered A36 Bonanza, shows off the type's elegant lines. The largest single-engine Beech, it was a six-seater and cruised at 193mph.

The improved Bonanza B36TC was introduced in 1981, with a 300hp Continental TS10-520-UB flat-six engine, a redesigned instrument panel, extra fuel capacity of 102 US gallons, increased wingspan and wedge-type vortex generators on the wing leading edges.

One of the smaller range of Beech aircraft was the Model 23 Musketeer introduced in 1962 for private and club use. The prototype (N948B) first flew on 23 October 1961 and production deliveries started in the autumn of 1962. Powered by a 160hp Lycoming O-320-D2B engine with a two-blade Sensenich propeller, the Musketeer had a fixed tricycle landing gear and a fuel capacity of sixty US gallons. Its top speed at sea level was 144mph and its cruising speed 135mph. This is a British-registered Musketeer I, G-ASJO, in 1968.

A total of 553 Beech Model 23 Musketeer Is were produced at Wichita. The aircraft's nose wheel was steerable via the rudder pedals. This is another Musketeer I seen as British-registered G-ASFB during 1965.

British-registered Beech A23-24 Musketeer Super III G-AXCJ, powered by a 200hp Lycoming 10-360-A2B with a two-blade fixed-pitch propeller. The A23-24 made its first flight on 19 November 1965 and apart from the engine was similar to the earlier A23A Musketeer Custom III. This photograph was taken in 1971.

This Beech Model A23-24 Musketeer Super III, also powered by a 200hp Lycoming 10-360-A2B, is seen in 1965 when registered 9M-ANT and owned by the Royal Singapore Flying Club. The total production of A23-24 Musketeer Super IIIs amounted to 363 aircraft.

The Beech Model C23 Musketeer appeared in 1970 with a widened cabin front and enlarged, reshaped cabin windows. During 1972 C23s were re-engined with a 180hp Lycoming O-360-A4G, a port side door was made standard and the name 'Sundowner' was officially adopted. This British-registered Model C23 is seen in 1971.

Formerly known as the C23 Musketeer, the Beech Sundowner 180 was designed as the basic four-seater version powered by a 180hp Lycoming O-360-A4K engine with a Sensenich two-blade fixed-pitch metal propeller. It had a fixed tricycle landing gear and a maximum cruising speed of 136mph at sea level. This Dutch-registered Sundowner (PH-MBR) is pictured in 1990.

A US-registered Beech Sundowner 180 (N2064L) in its element. Originally a C23 Musketeer Custom, it has a 180hp Lycoming O-360-A4G engine. Seating four and with a fixed tricycle landing gear, the Sundowner 180 was economical, quiet and pleasant to fly. However, production of Sundowner 180s was suspended in 1984.

This two-seat Model A23-19 Sport was introduced in 1965. It was an economical version of the A23 series with a 150hp Lycoming O-320-E2C engine. Just two cabin windows were fitted, as seen on this A23-19 Sport (F-BNOV) of the Touring Club de France in 1967.

The Beech Model B19 Sport 150 of 1970, with a 150hp Lycoming O-320-E2C, was a two- to four-seat sporting and training type. Fully aerobatic, it was passed for rolls, spinning, looping, Immelmann turns and other manoeuvres. After 1978 the Model 19 was named the Beech Sport 150, like this US-registered N2059L.

Akin to the Sundowner, the Beech B24R Sierra 200 differed in having a 200hp Lycoming O-360-A1B6, a retractable tricycle landing gear, a constant-speed, two-blade propeller and accommodation for up to six persons. It cruised at 158mph, the range being 790 miles. This is US-registered Sierra 200 N221OL.

After its introduction in 1972, when fifty-five were built, the B24R Sierra 200 proved popular with its four to six-passenger accommodation. When production ended in 1976, 299 had been built, but in 1977 work started on a further 345 updated C24R Sierra 200s. Here is Danish-owned B24R Sierra 200 OY-AJD.

The military Model 45/USAF T-34 Mentor was a late 1940s private venture, all-metal, high performance trainer by Beech. The prototype (N8591A) first flew on 2 December 1948 with a 205hp Continental E-185-8, a third prototype having a 225hp Continental E-225-8. USAF evaluation took place in 1950-1951 and the YT-34 beat its competitors and was accepted. In 1953, as the T-34A, it was ordered into production for USAF service. Seen here is the first YT-34, 50-735.

US Navy evaluation of the Beech T-34 resulted in a substantial order for T-34Bs powered by a 225hp Continental 0-470-13 engine. Delivery to the Navy began on 17 December 1954, a total of 423 T-34Bs being built. Some remained in Navy service until the late 1970s. Seen here is US Navy T-34B BuNo 140667.

The upgrading of two T-34B Mentors in 1973 resulted in the YT-34C (production T-34C) with a 715shp Pratt & Whitney PT6A-25 turboprop, the latest avionics, extra fuel capacity and armament on underwing hardpoints comprising 7.62mm mini-guns, napalm or GP bombs, or 2.75in rockets. Seen here in 1997 with Sharksmouth insignia is a US Navy Beech T-34C (BuNo 160501).

54

Export variants of the Beech Model 45 Mentor (B45) were either sold or licence-built in twenty-three countries worldwide, including the Middle East, South and Latin America, the Far East, Canada and Europe. This B45, with PT6A-25 turboprop, is pictured in 1979 as 7T-WPD of the Algerian Air Force.

The Beech Model 73 Jet Mentor emerged in 1955. It was based on the T-34 and used some components. A two-seat jet trainer for the Navy, it had a Continental J69-T-9 turbojet engine. The prototype, N134B, seen here, flew on 18 December 1955 but no production order was made.

PD 285, a Beech two-seat basic trainer prototype (N285BA), first flew on 6 February 1975. Aimed at civil flying clubs, the seats were side-by-side, a normal conventional tailplane was fitted and power was provided by a 100hp Continental engine. Tests resulted in the use of a T-tail for improved low-speed pitch control and a replacement 115hp Avco Lycoming O-235-L2C engine. The first production machine flew on 12 September 1978 as the Model 77 Skipper. After 312 were built, production was suspended. The revised prototype Skipper is seen here on a test flight.

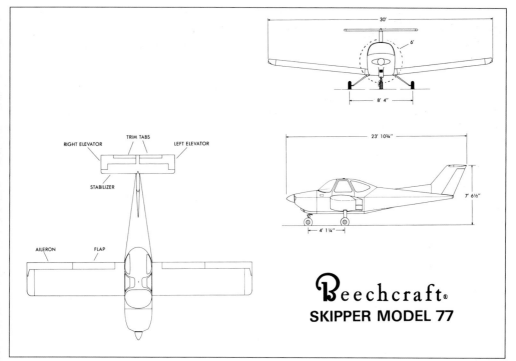

Plan views of the Model 77 Skipper.

The Beech Model 50 Twin Bonanza first flew on 15 November 1949 and used many Model 35 Bonanza components. US Army evaluation as the YL-23 resulted in orders for L-23As and L-23Bs. Early civil types were the A50 (1953), B50 (1954) and C50 (1955). Here Australian C50 VH-COE is seen in 1969 with Nicholas Skyways.

Powered by two 275hp Lycoming GO-480-F6 engines, the Beech C50 Twin Bonanza was introduced during 1955 in competition with the Aero Commander 560. Total production of civil C50s was 250 of which 216 were built in 1955 and the rest in 1954 and 1956. This C50 Twin Bonanza is with TOA Airways, Japan, in 1969.

The Model D50 Twin Bonanza of 1956 had minor air-frame and systems updating, three-blade Hartzell propellers and two 295hp Lycoming GO-480-G2F6 engines. This Twin Bonanza D50, N3694B, was with Spernak Airways Inc., Alaska Indian Line, as seen here in 1974.

This Twin Bonanza D50 (N99888), photographed around 1977, has the American national flag painted across its fin and rudder. The pair of Lycoming GO-480-G2F6s are fitted with Hartzell three-blade propellers.

Very similar to a Twin Bonanza D50, the D50E had two Lycoming GO-480-G2F6 engines. These provided 285hp at 3,100rpm (normal) and 295hp at 3,400rpm (take-off). The French D50E F-BLEG is seen here on its home territory in 1967.

An interesting hangar scene with a French-registered Beech D50E (F-BKBN), its cowlings raised for maintenance on its partly revealed Lycoming GO-480-G2Fs. Note the starboard-mounted entrance and steps.

A Beech Twin Bonanza Model E50 of 1957, with two 340hp supercharged Lycoming GSO-480-A1A6 engines. January 1957 saw deliveries commence of the military L-23D version. Some US Army L-23Ds became RL-23Ds (later RU-8Ds) fitted with AN/APS-85 or AN/APQ-86 for all-weather battleground surveillance. This E50 (A-713) is seen in 1985 with the Troupe d'Aviation Helvetique (Swiss Air Force).

After a rigid flight test programme of the Model 50 Beech Twin Bonanza prototype (N3992N), eleven air-frames were completed in 1952 as pre-production machines for civil and military use. The US Army ordered four YL-23s as general and staff personnel transports, followed by fifty-five L-23As (named 'Seminole') for service in Korea. One of the original YL-23s, A52-1801, is seen here with 260hp Lycoming GO-435-C2 engines. It was later brought up to L-23A (U-8A) standard as a Seminole.

From the first production batch of L-23As this US Army Seminole (52-6164) with 260hp GO-435-17 engines and two-blade wooden propellers accommodated up to six personnel and had provision for Rocket Assisted Take-Off Gear (RATOG). It would later be rebuilt as an L-23D with refinements and uprated engines.

This L-23A Seminole (52-6162) was the first of the initial fifty-five production machines ordered in 1952 for use in the Korean War. It would eventually become a revised L-23D (U-8D in 1962) with 340hp Lycoming GSO-480-B1B6 engines, but is pictured here at Fort Meade in its original form in 1958.

A Beech RL-23D Seminole (later RU-8D), US Army No.58-1361 was a radar-equipped version of the L-23D. The APS-85 radar or APQ-86 SLAR was carried in a ventral pod and some had nose-mounted AN/AVQ-50 or similar weather radar system. The engines are 340hp Lycoming O-480-1s driving Hartzell three-blade propellers.

Initially a Beech RL-23D, but U-8G after 1962, this US Army machine (58-1348) is fitted with a ventral 'Project Michigan' containing an AN/UPD-1 blister airborne radar system. The aircraft was powered by 340hp Lycoming O-480-1 piston engines and is shown around 1959-1960.

Pictured here in 1979 is a Beech U-8D (ex-L-23D) Seminole serving with the US Army/National Guard, Vermont. Its engines are 340hp Lycoming O-480-G2D6s with Hartzell three-blade propellers. The full US Army serial is 57-6059.

This special version of a Beech RU-8D (ex-RL-23D), US Army No.58-1360, is an electronic intelligence aircraft (ELINT) equipped with AN/APQ-85 side-looking airborne radar (SLAR) in a ventral pod and nose-mounted AN/AVQ-50 weather radar. Based on the Model E50, this variant was also powered by two 340hp Lycoming O-480-A1A6 supercharged engines.

In order to provide an intermediate aircraft between their single-engined Model 35 Bonanza and six-seat Model 50 Twin Bonanza, Beech produced the Model 95 Travel Air four-seat executive aircraft. Its cabin was well endowed with windows, while power was provided by two 180hp Lycoming O-360-A1A engines. A tricycle landing gear was electrically-operated and Beech air-oil shock absorbers fitted. The first flight of the prototype Travel Air was on 6 August 1956. The B95 variant of 1960 had a 19in-longer cabin plus greater empennage area including a new dorsal fairing. This machine carries the Swiss registration HB-GCA.

The name Travel Air was adopted for the Model 95 as a tribute to the well-known biplanes of the 1920s which earned fame for Walter H. Beech. This Model B95A of 1961 had fuel-injected Lycoming IO-360-B1As giving a higher speed. Carrying Danish registration OY-AOP, this B95A Travel Air was G-ASZC in the UK.

Seen here in Finland during the 1970s is Finnish-registered B95A Travel Air OH-BTA, with a pair of fuel-injected 180hp Lycoming IO-360-B1A engines. At first the Model 95 was named Badger but in order to avoid confusion with the USAF code name Badger for the Tu-16 Russian bomber, it was changed to Travel Air.

When the D95A Travel Air emerged in 1963 it had a revised, more tapered nose containing an enlarged luggage area plus most of the radio equipment, an increased weight limit for the rear cabin baggage and better interior styling. This D95A Travel Air, G-ASMF, is seen with Everton Engineering Ltd in 1964.

A smart-looking Beech Model D95A Travel Air with UK registration G-ATLX in 1967. The more tapered nose and ample window space are apparent in this view. Engines are 180hp Lycoming IO-360-B1Bs driving 6ft diameter Hartzell propellers. The wheels, brakes and fuel injection system were all updated on the D95A.

In 1974 Beech launched a new twin-engine, four-seat cabin monoplane with a T-tail and cantilever low wing. Powered by two 180hp Lycoming O-360-A1G6Ds, it was extensively tested before entering production as the Model 76 Duchess in 1978. Here a new Duchess is on test from Beechcraft's Liberal plant, Kansas.

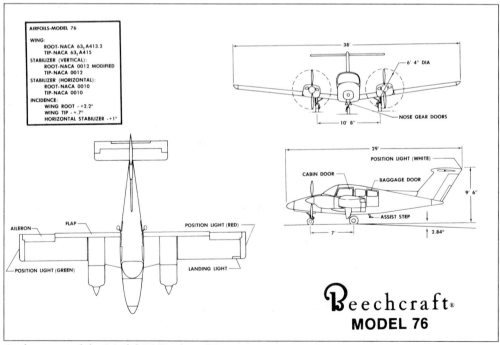

A plan view of the Model 76 Duchess 76.

The Beech Model 76 Duchess accommodated four people, two in front seats with reclining backs and two on a bench-type seat behind. It would make an ideal multi-engine trainer, but was offered as either a Week-ender, Holiday or Professional. Several details are clear on this photograph of British-registered Duchess G-OADY.

During 1967 Beech introduced the Model 99 Airliner accommodating two crew and fifteen passengers. It was designed as a light transport and third-level airliner or air taxi and evolved from a 'stretched' Model 65 Queen Air test bed. Among the first Beech 99 operators was Allegheny Airlines: two of their aircraft are seen here in the 1980s. The nearest (N133CA) is an improved B99 while the next machine (N99CH) is a Model 99.

Production of Model 99 Airliners began in 1966 and on 2 May 1968 initial deliveries went to Commuter Airlines Inc. A substantial number of foreign airlines ordered Beech Model 99 Airliners, starting with Australia, Canada and Mexico. By June 1969 over thirty-two foreign airlines were flying Beech 99s. Pictured here as late as 1996 is VH-OXB, a Model 99 operated by the Australian Impulse/Ansett airline.

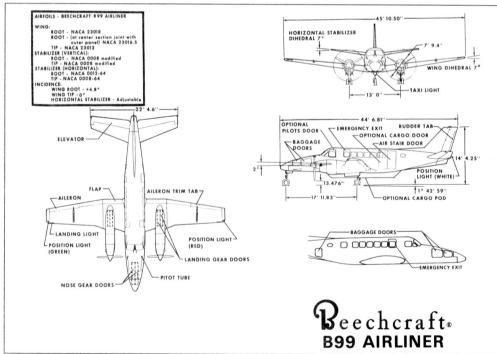

This company plan of the B99 from 1978 clearly shows the long cabin with its emergency exits on each side.

The Model 99 Airliner was powered by two 550shp Pratt & Whitney PT6A-20 turboprops with three-blade, constant-speed, reversible-pitch propellers. Pictured here is the improved Model B99, which was heavier with uprated 680shp PT6A-28 engines and is shown with an optional ventral cargo pod fitted. This machine (N4299A) was a Beech demonstration aircraft.

Seen here in 1969 is a Beech Model 99 Airliner in Aero Commuter colours. This machine (N9995) has been fitted with the optional ventral cargo pod. The fin and rudder feature a painted clock face and the logo 'Timesaver Jet'. The extreme nose artwork depicting a time element is also noteworthy.

Operating in colder latitudes was this Beech Model 99 Airliner, LN-SAL, of Nordsjofly, Norway, seen here in 1977. Baggage doors are located in the nose on both sides and the emergency exit is clearly marked around each front cabin window. The air-stair door can be seen lowered on the port side.

Four
Sky Queen –
The Beech Queen Airs

In order to meet demand for a twin-engined business aircraft, Beech produced a development of the Twin Bonanza. Known as the Model 65 Queen Air, it sat seven to nine people and embodied some modern airliner features. It had a low cantilever wing and was powered by two 340hp Lycoming IGSO-480-A1B6 fuel-injected, supercharged piston engines. The prototype N821B first flew on 28 August 28 1958. French-registered F-BMLD is seen here in 1967.

The Beech Model 65 Queen Air used Hartzell three-blade, fully-feathering, constant-speed propellers and its fuel capacity was 230 US gallons contained in main and auxiliary wing tanks. This 1967 photograph shows LN-NPP, a Norwegian-registered Model 65 Queen Air of the 'West Wing' company.

The latest contemporary electronics and instrumentation for all-weather operations were incorporated into the Beech Model 65 Queen Air, while optional radar and radio systems, oxygen gear, autopilot and extra soundproofing were available. This Dutch Model 65, PH-ILS, is seen in 1967 operated by Philips Nv.

The alternative use as a cargo aircraft was achieved in the Beech 65 Queen Air by removing the bulkheads and passenger seats to give 266cu.ft of cargo space. In this 1966 view is British-registered Model 65 G-AROU, which was owned by the Kenwood Group of companies.

Like other Beech types, the Model 65 Queen Air sold abroad in some numbers. Here Australian-registered VH-SLB is seen in 1968 when operating with the Swan Brewery Group as an executive transport. Note the lowered air-stair on the port side and the swan motif on the fin. Altogether, 316 Model 65 Queen Airs were built for the civil market.

Basically similar to a Model 65, the improved A65 appeared in 1967 with sweptback tail surfaces, a total fuel capacity of 264 US gallons (including auxiliary wing tanks) and Lycoming IGSO-480-A1E6 engines. In this 1980 photograph, a Beech Model A65 Queen Air is shown serving with H.Q. Squadron of the Japanese Maritime Self Defence Force (JASDF).

An updated Queen Air Model A80 of 1964 (normally known as the Queen Air 80). It followed the 65-80 of 1961, retaining that variant's swept tail and more powerful 380hp IGSO-540-A1A engines. This Model A80, British-registered G-ASRX, is with Martin Baker Ltd in 1967, but within a year it was owned by Pye.

Another update on the Model A80 was a greater wing-span of 50ft 3in, as well as a revised nose section, increased gross weight and an extra thirty-four US gallons of fuel capacity. Basking in South African sunshine here in 1972 is a Beech Model A80 registered ZS-UAS and belonging to South Africa's United Air.

The twin 380hp Lycoming engines that powered the Beech Model A80 were fitted with Hartzell three-blade propellers as seen on this French-registered machine, F-BMCX, with Rousseau Aviation (note the initials RA on the rudder).

A number of Model A80s were purchased by foreign air arms. This machine, the only example sold to the People's Socialist Republic of the Union of Burma, carries that country's national insignia and serial number UB380. Note the air-stair open on the port side.

Australia also received a number of Beech Queen Air A80s, like this one registered VH-BQL and owned by Coddair Airlines. It is worth noting that Beech did propose a Model A80-8800 (originally Model 89) with specified airliner interior and a gross weight of 8,800lb. In the event, 121 A80 Queen Airs were built.

The Australian Flying Doctor Service is well known, but back-up for serious cases is available by means of ambulance aircraft, in this case VH-AMG, a Beech A80 of the New South Wales Ambulance Service, in around 1984.

During 1966 Beech introduced the Model 65-B80 Queen Air, an update of the A80 with IGSO-540-A1A engines instead of the -540-A1Ds but retaining the 50ft 3in wingspan. This 1967 photograph is of French-registered Beech Queen Air B80 F-BMCX owned by Air Affaires.

Altogether, 242 Model B80s were produced, including a few B80As with lower-powered engines. A number went abroad like this French-registered Model B80, F-BMMC, seen here in 1967.

In South America the Colombian Air Force purchased three Beech Model B80s. This one, LD230/'IGM', was with Escuadron de Transporte 412 of Grupo 41 based at Barranquilla. The legend along the upper fuselage reads 'Instituto Geográfica Militar' and the name below the cockpit, *Condor 1*. The photograph dates from around 1977.

To increase useful payload at reasonable operating costs, Beech produced the Model 70 Queen Air/Queen Airliner. It incorporated the 340hp Lycomings of the Model A65 and the 50ft 3in wingspan of the Model 80 and was aimed at commuter airlines. Seen here in 1970 is US-registered N4071A of Masling Airlines.

The Beech Model 70 carried up to nine passengers. A ventral cargo pod, air conditioning and a large cargo door were optional. Of thirty-five Beech Model 70s built, eleven were sold to the Société de Travail Aérien (STA) of Algeria. This STA machine (7T-VSL) is pictured in 1969.

The Beech Model 88 Queen Air was a pressurized form with circular windows introduced in 1965. A piston-engined variant of the Model 90 King Air turboprop at a reduced price, it had a pair of 380hp Lycoming IGSO-540-A1Ds and cruised at 221mph. This Queen Air 88 is carrying German registration D-ILKI and is seen in 1967.

US Army requirements for a revised U-8 Seminole in 1958 resulted in the Beech L-23F (U-8F from 1962). A Model 50 with increased cabin height, three large cabin windows, a new interior and 340hp Lycomings, it carried ten personnel or seven fully armed troops. U-8F Seminole No.62-3870 is seen here in Vietnam in 1967.

Similar to civil Beech Model B80s, the US Army U-21A had 550shp Pratt & Whitney PT6A-20 turboprops and contained electronics, navigation aids and de-icing gear for all-weather duties. This U-21A (66-18000) was the first production aircraft, later converted to an EU-21A electronic reconnaissance aircraft.

This 1990 shot is of a Beech RU-21A (a converted U-21A), US Army No.67-18115 of N.G. FI 138 ASA. It was one of four U-21As (67-18112/18115) converted for electronic reconnaissance/interception. This machine is carrying wingtip tanks.

Another RU-21A of US Army N.G. Fl 138 ASA, this is the second of the four U-21A conversions, No.67-18113, also with wingtip tanks. Its engines were 550shp Pratt & Whitney PT6A-20 turboprops giving a maximum speed of 265mph at 10,000ft.

With different equipment and antenna array this was the Beech RU-21C of which only two were built. This is No.67-18085 of US Army N.G. Fl 138 ASA in 1990.

Five
Of Barons, Dukes and Kings

In November 1960 Beech launched the Model 55 Baron to succeed the Model 95 Travel Air. The wings were still basically the same as on the Travel Air, but a swept-back fin and rudder, two 260hp Continental IO-470-L engines, updated avionics and blind-flying equipment were all standard on the four-to five-seat Model 55. Over 300 Model A55 Barons followed – six-seaters (optional) with improved landing gear extension speed. This A55 Baron is seen in 1967 as Dutch-registered PH-ILP with Philips Nv.

After appearing in 1962, the Beech Model A55 Baron became very popular and over 300 were built in 1962-1963. Here a US-registered A55 Baron (N821B) is seen in the 1970s.

Eleven Beech Model 95-A55 and B55 Baron business aircraft were entered on the British civil aircraft register. Seen here is the Iliffe 'Flight International' A55 G-ASDO, pictured on a wet day in 1967.

The updated Model B55 Baron of 1964 incorporated a lengthened nose, which increased baggage space by fifty per cent. Gross weight was up by 120lb and for an improved climb rate the aircraft was fitted with new Beech two-blade, constant-speed propellers. Seen here is US-registered Baron B55 N17655, cruising at around 216mph.

Awaiting its next flight is US-registered Beech B55 Baron N1469G of Winship Air Service, from Anchorage, Alaska. Note the longer nose on this version providing additional baggage space. Two 260hp Continental IO-470-L engines provide the power.

A military version of the B55 Baron was designated T-42A and named the Cochise. This aircraft went to the US Army, as well as the Turkish and Spanish Air Forces. Pictured here in 1989 is a Spanish Air Force T-42A Cochise, No.E20-7/'42-64' of Ala 42.

The Beech Model C55 Baron appeared in August 1965. It featured a lengthened fuselage, a revised, one-piece windscreen, a wider span tailplane (15ft 11in), minor interior updates and more powerful 285hp Continental IO-520-C engines. This C55 Baron is German-owned D-ICDA. In 1967 twelve C55 Barons were acquired by The College of Air Training at Hamble, UK, for British airline crew training.

Seen here at an air show in 1967 is British-owned Beech Model C55 Baron G-AVET belonging to Eagle Air Services. The longer fuselage on this variant is apparent as are the spacious windows to give an excellent field of view for crew and passengers.

With the same 285hp Continental IO-520-C engines as the C55 and D55 Baron (the D55 basically identical to the C55 but with vacuum instead of pneumatic pressure), the E55 Baron had a modified interior and minor updates. This US-registered E55 Baron (N17845) is riding the clouds in style.

Beech introduced a very much updated Baron in 1969 as the Model 58. It kept to a Model 36 cabin but had E55 wings, two 285hp Continental IO-520-Cs, a fuel capacity increase (from 1976), double passenger/cargo doors (in 1984), longer propeller hubs, revised engine nacelles and a fourth window on each side of the cabin. This is US-registered Baron 58 N63858 over rugged US terrain.

The Beech Baron 58 featured 'wet' wingtips from 1976, thus increasing fuel capacity by twenty-eight US gallons. It featured one of the largest cabins among light twin-engine types, had an oxygen installation for high altitude and cruised at 230mph. Here a US Baron 58 (N9049V) shows off its aesthetic profile.

Beech Model 58 Barons were very popular both in the US and abroad, with production continuing throughout more than two decades so that by 1995 over 1,675 had been built. Here French-registered Baron 58 F-BSEF is pictured in 1990. The motif on the nacelle reads 'La Cino'/5 accompanied by a star.

Powered by two 310hp Continental TS10-520-LBIC engines, this pressurized version of the Baron 58 was designated Model 58P. Its first flight was on 16 August 1973. Standard six-seat accommodation was provided, as well as double doors on the port side. In 1976 the fuel capacity was increased by twenty-four US gallons. Here a Baron 58P cruises above typical American open country.

The Beech Baron 58P, designed for efficient corporate transportation, performs its task well. Six persons are conveyed in pressurized comfort at up to 25,000ft altitude and speeds up to 277mph. Here US-registered N4477W is in its element.

Pilot's view of the instrument panel and controls in a Beechcraft Baron Model 58P. From 1977 the 58P's engines were two 325hp Continental TSIO-520-WBs. A three position flap pre-select control switch was fitted, fuel tank selection was made easier and there was a wide choice of customer-installed avionics.

Beech Baron Model 58P G-BNUN of British Midland. The length of the Continental TSIO-520-WB engines is apparent. A baggage door is in the nose, while entry to the front starboard cabin door is via an assist step and wing walkway. Access to the rear port passenger door is similar with an assist step and small walkway.

An updated version of the Model 58P flew on 31 October 1975 as the Baron 58TC, with turbo-supercharged 310hp Continental TSIO-520 engines. Flap operation was revised, with a three-position, pre-select control switch, and the seats, all forward facing, had shoulder harnesses fitted as standard equipment. This Baron 58TC (N158TC) is a Beech-owned demonstrator.

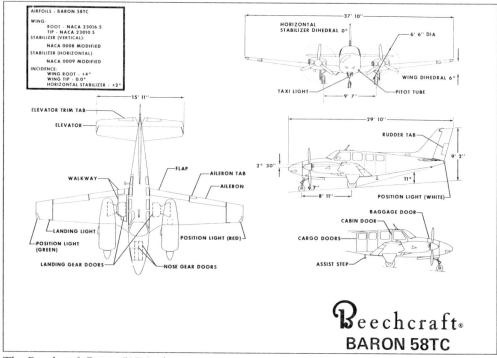

The Beechcraft Baron 58TC, showing the large double cargo doors on the starboard side.

In France, Sferma built a number of PD.146 Marquis aircraft using Baron airframes supplied by Beech. They were powered by two 450shp Turbomeca Astazou IIJ turboprops and flew from the 1960s to the 1980s. This German-registered Marquis (D-ILCA) is seen in 1967. Note the redesigned fin and propeller turbines.

To investigate the possibility of a pressurized aircraft powered by a single turboprop engine, in 1981 Beech converted a twin-engine Model 58P Baron to be powered by a single 550shp Garrett AiResearch TPE-331-9 turboprop. Registered N336BA, designated Model 38 and named *Lightning*, this one-off made its initial flight on 14 November 1983.

An aesthetically pleasing new design from Beech made its first flight on 29 December 1966. Known as the Model 60 Duke, it was a four to six-seater powered by a pair of turbo-supercharged 380hp Lycoming TIO-541-E1A4 engines. Fully pressurized and with advanced styling, it was an all-weather type cruising at around 271 to 275mph with a ceiling of 31,300ft. Here US-registered Duke N9743S shows off its elegant lines and advanced aerodynamic qualities.

Another US-registered Beech Model 60 Duke, N7034D seen in 1979. The retractable tricycle landing gear was electrically operated, while the standard fuel capacity was 142 US gallons, although four optional wing tanks raised this to 204 US gallons.

In the Beech Model 60 Duke, air from the turbo-supercharged engines could pressurize the cabin to 4.6psi, which gave sea-level conditions to 10,000ft altitude and a 10,000ft cabin altitude at 24,800ft. This Beech Model 60 Duke is an Austrian-owned aircraft, OE-FFD, pictured in 1970.

Seating arrangements on the Model 60 Duke consisted of four individual seats located in pairs with a centre aisle. Fifth and sixth seats were offered as optional extras. Here a French-registered Duke (F-BRSC) rests on a snow-covered surface.

The updated Model B60 Duke appeared in 1974, with Lycoming TIO-541-E1C4s, an enlarged cabin and improved seats. A revised pressure system was introduced along with wet-cell wingtip tanks (thirty US gallons) which gave the B60 Duke a 1,287 mile range. Here US-registered B60 Duke N9743S reveals the type's graceful form.

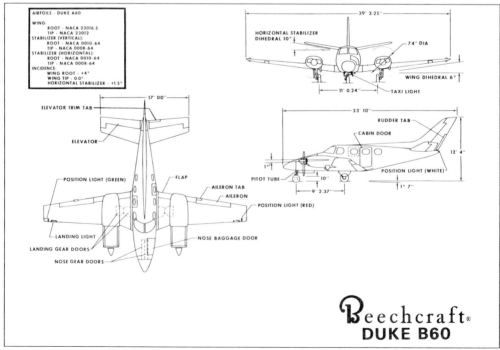

These Beechcraft promotional plan views of the B60 Duke show the long sweep up from the fuselage to the tail fin that gives the type its distinctive style.

One of the best-known Beechcraft types is the King Air series, which originated as an outgrowth of the piston-engined Queen Air via the military NU-8F with its Pratt & Whitney PT6A turboprops. A production prototype Model 65-90 King Air (N5690K) flew on 24 January 1964 with 550shp PT6A-6 engines. The improved Model A90 of 1966 had PT6A-20 engines, a fuel capacity of 384 US gallons and an improved pressurization system. It first flew on 5 November 1965. Here is a Canadian-registered King Air A90, CF-CGJ.

First flown on 13 April 1967, the updated Beech King Air B90 had 550shp Pratt & Whitney (UACL) PT6A-20 turboprops and incorporated a number of improved systems. Here British-registered and GKN-owned King Air B90 G-AXFE rests on the grass with its crew at an air show in the 1980s. Note the position of the door and the lowered air-stair door.

A total of 184 B90 King Airs were produced between 1967 and 1970, their PT6A-20 turboprop engines driving Hartzell three-blade, constant-speed, fully feathering propellers. The top speed was 270mph and the cruising speed 253mph. Here at a 1980s air show is German-registered B90 King Air D-ILTO.

Introduced in September 1970, the Beech C90 King Air featured an increase in wingspan and PT6A-21 turboprop engines. Here, with its air-stair lowered, is British-registered G-RCCL, a C90 King Air owned by Reckitt & Colman, in a photograph from the 1980s.

Like other Beechcraft types, the King Airs sold well abroad and four C90s went to the Spanish Air Ministry's Civil Aviation School. This C90, EI-BLI, was acquired in Ireland (Eire) and flown by Avair.

Eighteen Beech Model C90 King Airs were delivered to the Japanese Military Self Defence Force (JMSDF) for service with 202 Kyoiku Kokutai (Squadron) at their Tokushima base. Here one of these machines is numbered 6804 on the fin/rudder with the squadron number above it.

Resting in English sunshine is Beech C90 King Air G-PTER, owned by Colt Executive Aviation. The writing beneath the cockpit window reads 'Bright Eyes IV'.

The Model 90 King Airs sat six to ten people, and the C90-1 variant, which first flew on 29 September 1970, had a gross weight of 9,650lb, a 384 US gallon fuel capacity and pressurization of 5psi. Seen here in 1984 is C90-1 King Air G-BKIP, owned by Reckitt & Colman Products Ltd, Norwich, UK.

Major updates were introduced on the C90A King Air: new 'pitot' cowlings for improved efficiency and to reduce drag, state-of-the-art electrics, a new type of hydraulically actuated landing gear extension and retraction, plus a number of other modifications. This 1985 photograph shows British-registered C90A G-BKUX in service with the McAlpine company.

The first flight of the C90A King Air was on 1 September 1983, its improved cowling air intakes and tapered stacks all helping to reduce drag and improve engine efficiency. A rudder boost system eases handling if only one engine is operating. Here the new cowling features are apparent on US-registered C90A N66775.

On 1 May 1972 the Model E90 King Air was announced, retaining the C90 airframe but powered by 680ehp PT6A-28 turboprops and with a standard fuel capacity of 474 US gallons. Fully pressurized, it carries up to ten people and has a top speed of 287mph. This E90, G-BGNU, belonged to Norwich Union at the time the photograph was taken.

A 'go anytime, go anywhere' type of aircraft, the King Air E90 has the capacity to carry ten people over a maximum cruising range of 1,295 miles. The state-of-the-art avionics installation includes an RCA AVC-111A main VHF transceiver and B3 antenna. Here King Air E90 N44KA unloads its passengers. Note the high gloss finish apparent beneath the port wing.

A nice three-quarter rear shot of US-registered King Air E90 N64RA, owned as an executive aircraft by Reading Alloys, which has its motif in an oval across the fin and rudder. The tailplane dihedral is noticeable in this photograph.

A number of King Air Model 90s flew with military air arms abroad. Venezuela received five Model 90s for its Air Force (Guardia Nacional) and one E90 for the Venezualan Navy (Marina), seen here and serialled TR-0201.

Originally flown in America as N60253, this Beech King Air Model E90 was sold to an Irish buyer and registered EI-BHL. Note the exhaust stacks connected to the lower propeller blades. In total, 347 King Air E90s were produced, the last six in 1981.

When it appeared in 1979, the updated Beech King Air Model F90 featured the fuselage and wings of an E90 with the T-tail of a King Air Model 200. Power was also uprated by having two 750shp Pratt & Whitney PT6A-135 turboprops installed driving four-blade, constant-speed, fully feathering, reversible propellers, an aid to reducing noise level. Including the prototype, 203 King Air F90s were built. This one is British-registered G-STYR of Colt Executive Aviation. Below the cockpit the writing reads 'Bright Eyes II'.

T-tail style empennage is well displayed on this Beech King Air Model F90. This variant incorporated a much advanced electrical system. Here is a King Air F90 with Danish registration OY-BEL, belonging to the famous Lego company.

Prominent here are the four-blade, constant-speed, fully feathering, reversible propellers driven by two 750shp Pratt & Whitney PT6A-135 turboprops on this Beech King Air F90, US-registered N91P. Note the small 'acorn' at the junction of the fin and the T-tailplane.

Registered here as HI-449 is a Beech King Air F90 of the Dominican Republic, with PT6A-135 engines and four-blade propellers. Note the shape and position of the lowered wing flaps.

The updated Beech F90-1 first flew in December 1982 with PT6A-135A turboprops flat-rated at 750shp but having a high standard-day thermodynamic rating of 885shp at maximum continuous take-off power. Here F90-1 N14KA shows off its revised engine cowlings with their new frontal areas to improve performance. Increased fuel tankage was also incorporated.

A military version of the Beech Model 90 King Air was the US Army's U-21A (Model A90-1C) with 550shp PT6A-20s. Unpressurized, the U-21A had a combined cargo/air-stair door and squared-off cabin windows. This U-21A is seen when serving as No.8 with NASA.

Four Beech Model A90-1s were converted for US Army Security Agency use as electronic warfare machines and designated RU-21As. They were serialled 67-18112/18115, this being the third aircraft, 67-18114. Notice the wingtip tank and antenna atop this RU-21A.

The US Navy version of the Beech Model 90 was the H90 of 1976, designated T-44A (for multi-engine advanced trainer). Powered by PT6A-34Bs, some thirty-eight T-44As were ordered by the Navy with deliveries commencing in April 1977 to Training Wing Four at the NAS Corpus Christi, Texas. The Beechcraft T-44A (H90) shown here is BuNo 160980/'D' of US Navy Squadron VT-31.

After the first successful flight of its new Model 100 King Air on 17 March 1969, Beech introduced it officially on 26 May as an addition to its line of corporate transport aircraft. This version possessed a lengthened fuselage, shorter wingspan, larger tail surfaces, fences on the upper wing surfaces, dual-wheel main landing gear and uprated 680shp PT6A-28 turboprop engines. Among the interior alternatives was one for a fifteen-seat commuter, while up front an updated control pedestal and state-of-the-art avionics were standard. Shown is a German-registered King Air 100, D-IMSH, c.1979.

Beechcraft's King Air 100 had Hartzell three-blade, fully feathering, reversible-pitch, constant-speed propellers of 7ft 9in diameter. The pressurization system had a limited maximum differential of 4.7psi. Here Model 100 King Air N1800W stands outside one of Beechcraft's works in the 1970s.

The fuel system in the Beech King Air 100 featured new jet pumps, which replaced transfer pumps, and the wing-mounted rubber fuel cells had a total capacity of 374 US gallons. Beech King Air 100 LN-PAJ, owned by the Norwegian company Partnair, is seen here while waiting for its next flight. Note the elaborate decoration of the tail.

During 1971 the upgraded Beech Model A100 King Air entered production. It retained the PT6A-28 engines but had four-blade propellers which gave a maximum cruising speed of 285mph and a range of 1,384 miles (high cruise power with forty-five minutes reserve). This US-registered King Air A100, N928B, has its name, *The Free Enterprise*, written beneath its cockpit window.

Similar to the King Air A100, the Model B100 of 1975 had two 715shp Garrett AiResearch TPE-331-6 turboprops instead of the Pratt & Whitneys. Its maximum cruising speed was 306mph and its range 1,525 miles. The different profile of the Garrett engines can be seen in this photograph of US-registered N41KA.

Undoubtedly top of Beechcraft's company executive twin range of aircraft is the Super King Air series, evolved from the King Air 100 line but bearing only a superficial resemblance. The main difference is the Super King Air's T-tail, which keeps the tailplane well out of the wing down wash and propeller slip-stream. It also has an 8ft longer wingspan, increased cabin pressurization and extra fuel capacity (making a higher gross weight) to give a longer range. Here in landing configuration, its 850shp PT6A-41 turboprops throttled back, is British-registered Super King Air 200 G-CUKL, pictured in 1984.

The prototype Super King Air 200 (N38B) first flew on 27 October 1972 and production deliveries began in February 1974. A two-man crew and up to thirteen passengers are carried in pressurized comfort at 320mph for 1,710 miles. On test here is the Beech Super King Air 200 demonstrator N200KA.

With its twin 850shp Pratt & Whitney PT6A-41 Turboprop engines, the Beech Super King Air 200 became popular both in the USA and overseas. Here a Swedish-registered Super King Air 200, SE-IGV, is pictured when belonging to THS of Sweden in the 1980s. Note the company initials in a circle on the fin.

A number of Beech Super King Air 200s were British-owned, like this one, G-BKTI, operated by the TI Group. It has the Hartzell three-blade, constant-speed, fully feathering, reversible-pitch propellers. Note the lowered air-stair and the TI Group logo aft of it and across the vertical tail surfaces.

The adaptability of the Beechcraft Super King Air 200 interior for specialized duties is apparent in this hangar shot of Libyan-registered 5A-DDY, in use as an air ambulance. Note 'Air Ambulance' across the fin in Arabic and English with the crescent insignia above.

Another British-registered Beech Super King Air 200 was this Model A200, G-BMCA, seen when operating with Marchwiel Aviation Ltd in the 1980s and based at Halfpenny Green.

Flight testing began in 1979 of the Model 200T, a Super King Air 200 modified for maritime patrol duties. It was fitted with fifty US gallon wingtip fuel tanks for extra range, special observation windows, surveillance radar and photographic gear. This Beech Model 200T demonstrator is registered N2067D.

In 1974 Beech contracted to deliver thirty-four military Model 200s to the US army and US Air Force. Designated C-12As, they had 750shp PT6A-38 turboprops, two pilot operation and accommodation for eight personnel or alternative cargo. This C-12A (or Huron), US Army 73-22261, is seen with H.Q. US Army Europe (USAREUR) in the 1970s.

The US Navy version of the Super King Air 200, the UC-12B personnel/utility transport. Powered by 850shpPT6A-41 engines, it has a large cargo door. Of sixty-six UC-12Bs initially ordered, forty-nine went to the Navy and seventeen to the Marines. A dozen more UC-12Bs (Model A200C) were ordered in August 1985. This UC-12B, US Navy BuNo 161191, is pictured at Jacksonville NAS in 1997.

This Beech UC-12B (Model A200C) in US Marine Corps service is serialled BuNo 161194. Coded 'EZ', it is with USMC unit MWHS-4 in the 1980s and employed on staff and personnel transport duties. Note the covers on the lower propeller blades tied in unison with the engine air intake covers.

Overleaf: Introduced in March 1981, the Beech Super King Air B200 was generally similar to the Model 200 but had PT6A-42 turboprop engines for better cruise and altitude performance. In 1984 a 3,000psi hydraulic landing gear system replaced the electro-mechanical type and 98in McCauley propellers were fitted. Here B200 N3695B passes a typical US city skyline.

On 6 October 1981 a much updated Super King Air made its first flight as the prototype Model 300 (N4679M) powered by 1,050shp PT6A-60A turboprops driving four-blade Hartzell propellers. A top speed of 365mph was 27mph faster than the B200, while its gross weight was 14,000lb and it carried a standard-equipped useful load of 5,810lb. At maximum-range power, the Super King Air 300 can fly 1,960 nautical miles (2,255 statute miles) with reserves. The clean lines of the Model 300 are shown to advantage in this fine aerial shot of a Beech Super King Air 300 on a test flight.

Owing to the greater length of the Super King Air 300's uprated PT6A-60A engines, the position of the propellers is 5.2in further forward and there is a 5in forward extension of the inboard wing leading-edge. Pictured at rest with its air-stair lowered, this Swiss-owned Super King Air 300 is registered HB-GIP.

The Beech Super King Air 300 offered its owner the flexibility to fill fuel tanks, passenger seats and baggage space (550lb maximum) and still operate easily within the aircraft's centre-of-gravity and gross-weight limits. Seen here in 1997 is Austrian-registered Super King Air 300 OE-FME.

Readily identified by its engine 'pitot cowls' with 70sq.in of inlet area (the B200 has 88sq.in), which provides better ram recovery of inlet air, the Model 300 has an inlet efficiency of some 95%. This Super King Air 300 (N77) is seen in 1994 with the Federal Aviation Administration (FAA).

The cabin of a Super King Air 300 looking forward. This featured improved acoustics, thermal protection, good serviceability, aesthetic sensitivity and less weight. Single-piece upper side panels covered in a new soft-touch fabric replaced individual window frames, while a new overhead direct lighting system is fitted. Note the luxury upholstery and finish.

Designed primarily for the European market, the Beech Super King Air 30LW (LW for lightweight) was revealed in September 1988. The PT6A-60A turboprops are retained, the maximum take-off weight of this variant being 12,500lb. This Spanish-registered Super King Air 300LW (EC-FLX) is pictured in 1995.

The Beech Super King Air 350 of 1989 retained the PT6A-60As, but the wingspan was increased by 1ft 6in and the fuselage lengthened by 2ft 10in. Added winglets lessen drag at high altitude and help reduce stalling speed. Here in 1996 is a Swiss-registered Super King Air 350 (HB-GII) with ventral fins.

A good view here of the winglets incorporated into the wingtip of the Super King Air 350. An extra cabin window was also fitted and double club seating was provided for eight passengers (two optional seats could be added at the rear of the cabin). This is a French-owned Super King Air 350, F-GKIZ, in 1995.

The fuselage 'stretch' of the Beech Super King Air 350 was accomplished by inserting two plugs, one of 1ft 2in ahead of the main spar and one of 1ft 7in aft. The maximum take-off weight was 15,000lb carrying eleven passengers and a crew of two. This Model 350 is seen in 1993 as TC-SAB of Sabah Air, Turkey.

Six

Skyliners
and a Starship

In 1979 Beech began design work on a commuter airliner known as the Model 1900. A high-density layout was embodied in a 57ft 10in long fuselage, the wings comprising a new fail-safe structure featuring a continuous main spar without bolts. Power was in the form of two 1,100shp PT6A-65B turboprops driving four-blade Hartzell propellers. Three prototype Model 1900s were built, the first (c/n UA-1) making its initial flight on 3 September 1982. The subsequent production version was the 1900C, which had a large cargo door. This 1900C (F-GPYV) is with Air Littoral's Express service in France during 1997.

The first production Model 1900C was delivered in February 1984 and further orders quickly followed. By the summer of 1988, Beech 1900Cs were flying with eleven American and two European operators. This colourful example (N155GA) is with Grand Bahama Island Airline in 1998.

A corporate version of the Beech Model 1900C was produced as the 1900 Executive, known as the Exec-Liner. The first delivery of this variant went to the General Telephone Company of Illinois during the summer of 1985. Here 1900 Exec-Liner N6800J shows off its elegant plan form over a sparkling seascape.

A development of the Model 1900C is the 1900D with a deeper fuselage giving 28.5% more volume, a flat floor providing stand-up headroom and larger cabin windows and door. The crew of this US Airways Express 1900D (N857CA) are certainly relaxing before their next flight.

Uprated 1,280shp PT6A-67D turboprops power Beech 1900Ds, producing a maximum cruising speed of 330mph at 25,000ft. Twin ventral strakes are fitted as an aid to directional stability and can be seen on this 1900D, F-GRMD, of Proteus Airlines, France. The name, marked on the lower front, is *Ville De St Etienne*.

Note the four-blade Hartzell propellers, winglets at the wingtips, 'tail-lets' beneath horizontal tailplane and ventral strakes on Model 1900D VH-IMH of Australia's Impulse Airlines seen in 1999. The 1900 series also had 'stabilons' fitted to the rear fuselage below the fin. All these devices enhanced the aircraft's flight characteristics.

The innovative Beech Model 2000 Starship first flew as an 85% scale flying prototype on 29 August 1983 as seen here. An aft-mounted, laminar-flow wing, variable-sweep canard foreplane and two PT6A-60 turboprops in pusher configuration gave this aircraft a 'Star Wars' look. However, due to a poor market for the type, production ceased after some forty full-size production Starships had been built.